English edition first published 2019 by order of the Tate Trustees
by Tate Publishing, a division of Tate Enterprises Ltd,
Millbank, London SW1P 4RG
www.tate.org.uk/publishing

First published in French as *L'atelier Recup* © Mango jeunesse, Paris, 2017
This English edition © Tate 2019

A catalogue record for this book is available from the British Library

ISBN 978 1 84976 652 4

Distributed in the United States and Canada by ABRAMS, New York
Library of Congress Control Number applied for

Printed and bound in Latvia by Jelgavas

RECYCLING

Marie-Laure Pham-Bouwens & Steffie Brocoli

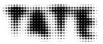

Marie-Laure Pham-Bouwens

I live in New York where I exercise my passion for the creative arts. I come up with activities, games and toys for children – and for adults, too! Working on these activities is fun and very satisfying – I am always proud of myself when I finish an object that I designed. And if it doesn't work, it doesn't matter, I just start again.

My favourite thing to do is to paint and create objects with recycled elements.

You will be able to find many other activities on my blog "The house of loulou".

I live and work in Paris as an illustrator of children's books, as well as for stationery and textiles. I create objects, paint large frescoes on walls, embroider flowers and much more!

I grew up in a family that likes to tinker and make things. When I was little, my dad taught me how to hammer nails into things to occupy myself! I love discovering and trying new techniques.

My dream would be to build sets and games for a funfair and amusement park for children!

Steffie Brocoli

CONTENTS

 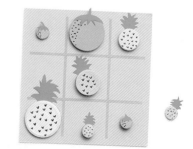

INTRODUCTION

In this book, there are eight brilliant activities
that you can do with recycled materials.

We will show you how to create beautiful objects for fun or to decorate your room with materials that you can find everywhere! Start collecting empty snack packages, cereal boxes, bottle caps – anything you think may come in handy! We will explain how to transform them in three illustrated steps. It takes a little material to paint or cut, but nothing complicated. If you do not have all the supplies, it doesn't matter! Swap painting for stuck on paper and vice versa, draw with a marker instead of a brush, uses decorated tape or stickers, add glitter – feel free and use whatever you have at home!

Some tips before you start:

• Choose a limited number of colours. In this book we chose four colours: blue, pink, green, yellow. We also use white or black for some details.
• When you want to paint an object, always paint a white undercoat first. The supports will absorb less paint and the colours will be brighter.
• Use acrylic paint so that multiple layers can be layered without mixing.
• Be sure to ask an adult for help when using scissors.

You can copy exactly what we have made for this book, or if you rather you may use your imagination and decorate these projects however you like!

Don't be afraid to make mistakes! If you don't like how your project turns out, you can start again very easily by repainting your object in white, or by making another one.

Ready your brushes and your scissors – it's time to start making!

MATERIALS and TOOLS

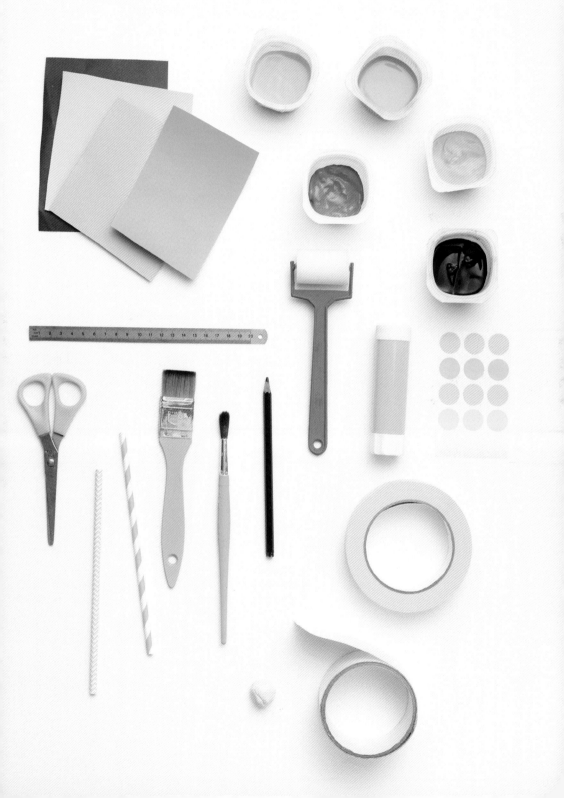

CARDBOARD CITY
with cardboard boxes

CARDBOARD CITY
with cardboard boxes

Save packages of different sizes –
cereal boxes, snack boxes,
toothpaste and more to create
your own cardboard city!

YOU WILL NEED

- empty boxes
- glue and tape
- a small roller and brushes
- acrylic paint

1

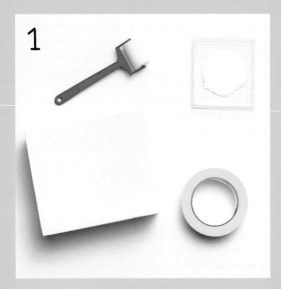

2

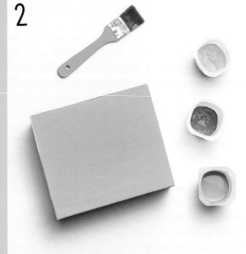

3

1. Close the openings of the box and tape
   them shut. Paint the box white with a
   roller and wait until it dries.
2. Next, paint the box with the colours of
   your choice. You can paint each box a
   different colour to add some fun to
   your city.
3. Now add some details: a door, a window,
   bricks, a tree – use your imagination! Do
   the same with boxes of different sizes.

Pile up the boxes to create your own city!

PAPER ANIMALS
with brown paper bags

PAPER ANIMALS

with brown paper bags

Use paper shopping bags or
small sandwich bags. If the bag
has handles, cut them off before
starting the activity!

YOU WILL NEED

- brown paper bags
- a pair of scissors
- glue
- acrylic paint
- a pencil

1

2

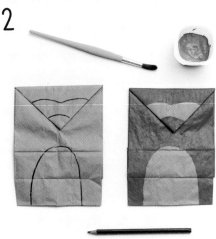

3

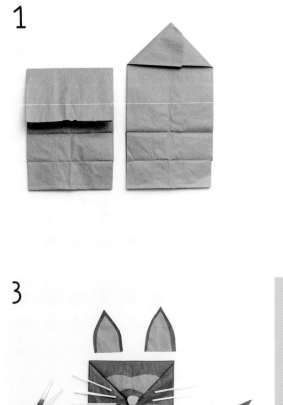

1. Fold down the top of the bag to make a
   line, then fold in the two top corners to
   make a triangle.
2. Fold the triangle down and draw out
   the face of your animal in pencil, then
   decorate it in paint. Let it dry.
3. Cut ears, whiskers, a tail and any other
   details you want to add from another
   brown bag, paint them, then stick them
   on to finish your paper animal!

Make a whole collection of different paper animals!

STACKABLE SCULPTURES
with cans

STACKABLE SCULPTURES

with cans

Do not throw away your cans, decorate them and collect them to make stackable structures! Before you begin, ask an adult to remove the lid and make sure there are no sharp edges . . .

YOU WILL NEED

- empty cans
- thick coloured paper
- a pair of scissors
- double sided tape
- acrylic paint
- paintbrushes

1

2

3

1. Paint the can white. Wait until it dries then paint it again with colour of your choice.
2. Choose a different coloured paper, then cut out wings, feathers and a small circle to hide the top of the can. Stick them on with double sided tape!
3. Paint on the other details – eyes, a beak, a mouth, patterns – anything you want!

You can now play with your sculptures, or even use them as a sculpture to decorate your room!

a little tip

Add some plastic googly eyes to make it even more fun!

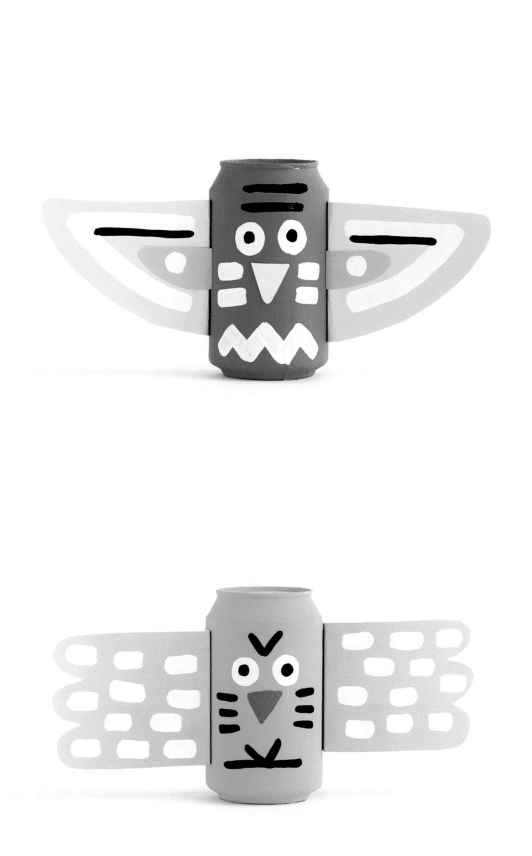

LITTLE ROCKETS
with cardboard tubes

LITTLE ROCKETS

with cardboard tubes

Collect rolls of toilet paper or paper towels to make super rockets!

YOU WILL NEED
- cardboard tubes
- coloured paper
- stickers
- aluminum foil
- double sided tape
- Scotch tape
- glue
- a compass
- a pair of scissors

1

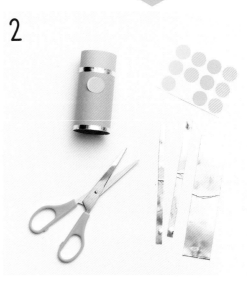

2

3

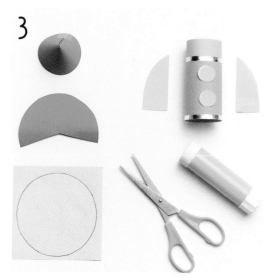

1. Cut out strips of paper (use the roll to measure) and glue them around your roll.

2. Add some stickers for the windows and cut out the wings. Glue aluminum foil onto paper with double sided tape to make silver sticky paper!

3. For the nose cone, cut a circle out of coloured paper, then cut a triangle shape out of it (as in the picture). Roll your paper in the shape of a cone and tape it closed, then fix it to the top of the rocket with some glue.

Your rocket is ready to launch!
1, 2, 3, blast-off!

a little tip

Use decorated adhesive to create
patterns on the wings.

You can also make small cars or planes with the cardboard rolls.

COOL MASKS
with egg boxes

COOL MASKS

with egg cartons

Use egg cartons to make a whole collection of masks! You can make three different masks with a box of six eggs.

YOU WILL NEED

- an empty egg box
- coloured paper
- acrylic paint
- paintbrushes
- a pair of scissors
- glue

1. Cut off the lid, and then cut out a section of the box to make a mask. Next, paint it white and let it dry.
2. Ask an adult to make holes for the eyes with a pair of scissors. Now decorate your mask with paint!
3. To make pretty feathers, fold your sheet of paper in half, cut a semicircle on the fold, then cut some nicks on the sides. Unfold, and your feather is finished! Now you can stick it on your mask.

You can hang your mask on your wall or add a rubber band to wear it and disguise yourself!

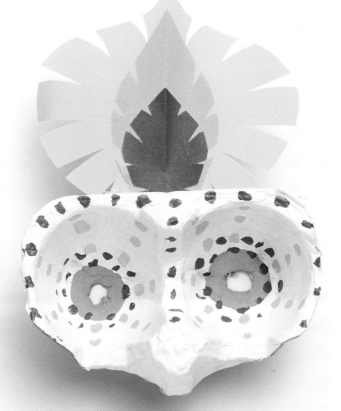

a little tip

Have fun making feathers of different sizes and stick them on top of each other!

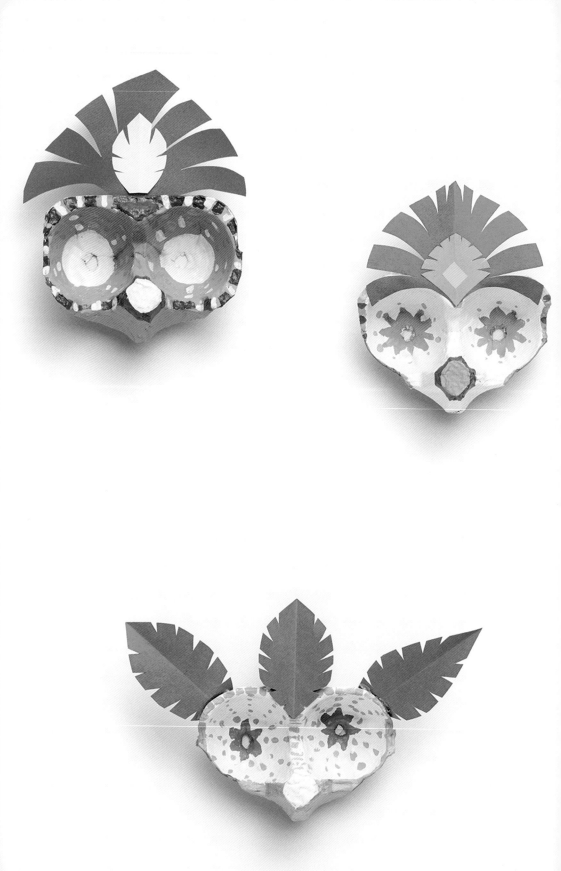

PAPER FLOWERS

with envelopes

PAPER FLOWERS

with envelopes

Have you ever noticed the patterns and different colours on the inside of some envelopes? Save used envelopes to make pretty paper flowers.

YOU WILL NEED

- used envelopes
- coloured paper
- one or more straws
- a pair of scissors
- invisible tape
- glue

1

2

3

1. Cut circles of different sizes out of saved envelopes and sheets of coloured paper.
2. Make cuts in your circles to make different types of petals. You can also cut out a small leaf for the stem.
3. Layer all the circles, (letting the petals show behind each other) and glue together to make your flower. With sticky tape, attach the straw to the back of your flower and add the leaf, wrapping it around the stem and glueing closed.

And now, your flowers are ready to be planted!

a little tip

You can also use a skewer or lollipop stick for the stem and magazine pages to make the petals!

E

A

STEFFiE BROCO

FUNNY ANIMALS
with milk cartons

FUNNY ANIMALS
with cartons

Collect empty milk or fruit juice cartons to make these little creatures! You can use them as pots for pencils or as secret treasure boxes...

YOU WILL NEED

- empty cardboard cartons
- paper straws
- acrylic paint
- a pair of scissors
- coloured papers
- blue-tac
- glue gun

1. Cut off the top of a cardboard carton and keep the bottom part. Paint it white, let it dry, then paint it in a nice bright colour.
2. Cut out some wings and antennae from the coloured paper, then fold one side to form a lip and stick them on to the box.
3. Decorate the body with paint. Cut the straws in half and stick them underneath with the blue-tac to make the legs. To make it stronger, you can ask an adult to fix them on with a glue gun.

There you go ! You can now garnish your box with sweets,
a little plant, pencils or little toys!

a little tip

You can use the plastic lids
from the carton for the nose!

TIC-TAC-TOE
with plastic lids

TIC-TAC-TOE
with plastic lids

Collect the plastic lids from cardboard cartons and the tops of bottles to make a game of tic-tac-toe! The caps can be different sizes.

YOU WILL NEED

- ten caps or lids
- acrylic paint
- paintbrushes
- a pair of scissors
- coloured papers
- cardboard and a ruler
- glue

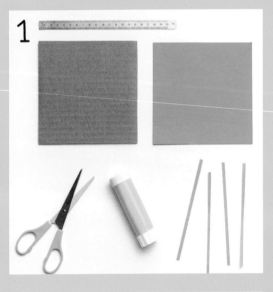

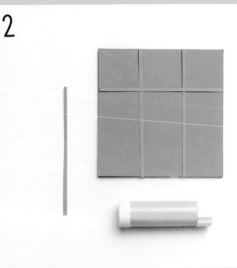

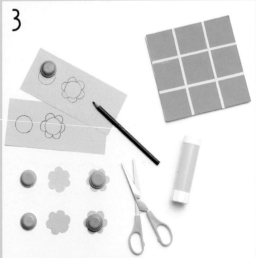

1. Cut a square out of cardboard, and a square of the same size in coloured paper. Cut out four thin strips of another piece of coloured paper.

2. Glue the paper square onto the cardboard, then glue your strips on top to form a grid. This will be your board.

3. Paint the ten caps in white, and once they are dry, paint five in one colour and five in another colour. Draw flowers larger than your caps on paper and cut them off. Glue your caps on top. Your game pieces are ready!

Tic-Tac-Toe or noughts and crosses is played by two people. The players pose in turn a pawn on the grid. The first one to line up three pieces in a row has won!

a little tip

You can replace the flowers with any pattern of your choice.

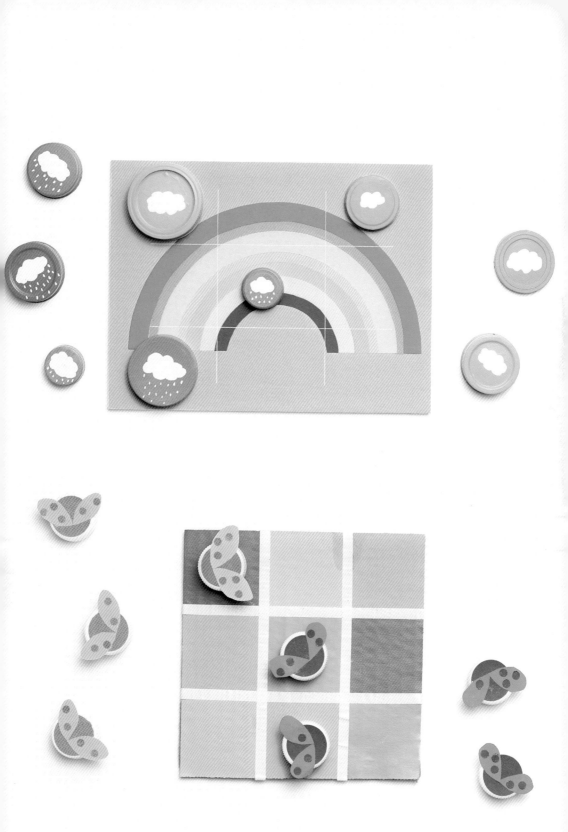

Each of the eight projects in this book are fun, easy-to-make
and will help you to build your crafting skills while
using your imagination to make wonderful things!

Every activity is an opportunity to decorate, use colour and design
your project in a way that makes it uniquely yours.

Why not show your friends how to make these projects too and share
them with each other? Seeing how other people use their imaginations is
a great way to get to know someone and find even more inspiration!

Always remember – safety first!

**Be sure to always let an adult know when you are about to use
scissors or glue, and always ask an adult for help when using a
craft knife – never use one on your own!**